THE RED BADGE
OF COURAGE

Stephen Crane

SPARKNOTES

Contributors: Brian Phillips, David Hopson, Valerie Jaffee

Copyright © 2002 by SparkNotes LLC

This edition published by Spark Publishing

Spark Publishing
A Division of SparkNotes LLC
76 9th Avenue, 11th Floor
New York, NY 10011

ISBN 1-58663-403-8

Text design by Rhea Braunstein
Text composition by Jackson Typesetting

Printed and bound in the United States of America

01 02 03 04 05 SN 9 8 7 6 5 4 3 2 1

RRD-C

http://www.sparknotes.com

Stopping to Buy SparkNotes on a Snowy Evening

Whose words these are you *think* you know.
Your paper's due tomorrow, though;
We're glad to see you stopping here
To get some help before you go.

Lost your course? You'll find it here.
Face tests and essays without fear.
Between the words, good grades at stake:
Get great results throughout the year.

Once school bells caused your heart to quake
As teachers circled each mistake.
Use SparkNotes and no longer weep,
Ace every single test you take.

Yes, books are lovely, dark, and deep,
But only what you grasp you keep,
With hours to go before you sleep,
With hours to go before you sleep.

CONTENTS

Stephen Crane was born in 1871 in Newark, New Jersey. The fourteenth child of highly religious Methodist parents, Crane lapsed into a rebellious childhood during which he spent time preparing for a career as a professional baseball player. After brief flirtations with higher learning at Lafayette College and Syracuse University, Crane turned to writing full-time. Convinced that he must invest his work with the authenticity of experience, he often went to outlandish lengths to live through situations that he intended to work into his novels. For his first book, *Maggie, a Girl of the Streets* (1893), Crane lived in poverty in the Bowery slum of New York City. Similarly, he based his short story "The Open Boat" on his experience as a castaway from a shipwreck.

Crane's most enduring work, the short novel *The Red Badge of Courage* was published in 1895. Though initially not well received in the United States, *The Red Badge of Courage* was a massive success in England. The attention of the English critics caused many Americans to view the novel with renewed enthusiasm, catapulting the young Crane into international literary prominence. His realistic depictions of war and battle led to many assignments as a foreign correspondent for newspapers, taking him to such locales as Greece, Cuba, and Puerto Rico. He published volumes of poetry as well as many works of fiction, including the landmark "The Open Boat" (1897). In 1899, Crane moved into a medieval castle in England with his lover, the former madam of a Jacksonville brothel. Here Crane wrote feverishly, hoping to pay off his debts. His health began to fail, however, and he died of tuberculosis in June 1900, at the age of twenty-eight.

Ironically, for a writer so committed to the direct portrayal of his own experience, Crane's greatest work is almost entirely a product of his imagination. When he wrote *The Red Badge of Courage,* Crane had neither fought in war nor witnessed battle, and was forced to rely on his powers of invention to create the extraordinarily realistic combat sequences of the novel. His work proved so accurate that, at the time of the book's publication, most critics assumed that Crane was an experienced soldier.

Based loosely on the events of the Civil War Battle of Chancellorsville (May 2–6, 1863)—though neither the battle, the war, nor the armies are named in the book—*The Red Badge of Courage* shattered American preconceptions about what a war novel could be. In the decades before Crane's novel, most fiction about the Civil War was heavily idealistic, portraying the conflict as a great clash of opposed ideals. Whereas previous writers had taken a large, epic view, Crane focused on the individual psychology of a single soldier, Private Henry Fleming, during his first experiences of battle. In this narrowed scope, Crane represents Henry's mind as a maze of illusions, vanity, and romantic naïveté, challenged by the hard lessons of war. Crane does not depict a world of moral absolutes, but rather a universe utterly indifferent to human existence.

This startling and unexpected shift drew the world's attention to *The Red Badge of Courage,* as did the novel's vivid and powerful descriptions of battle. With its combination of detailed imagery, moral ambiguity, and terse psychological focus, *The Red Badge of Courage* became hugely influential on twentieth-century American fiction, particularly the work of the modernists. These qualities continue to make the work absorbing and important more than a century after it was written.

During the Civil War, a Union regiment rests along a riverbank, where it has been camped for weeks. A tall soldier named Jim Conklin spreads a rumor that the army will soon march. Henry Fleming, a recent recruit with this 304th Regiment, worries about his courage. He fears that if he were to see battle, he might run. The narrator reveals that Henry joined the army because he was drawn to the glory of military conflict. Since the time he joined, however, the army has merely been waiting for engagement.

At last the regiment is given orders to march, and the soldiers spend several weary days traveling on foot. Eventually they approach a battle-field and begin to hear the distant roar of conflict. After securing its position, the enemy charges. Henry, boxed in by his fellow soldiers, real-izes that he could not run even if he wanted to. He fires mechanically, feeling like a cog in a machine.

The blue (Union) regiment defeats the gray (Confederate) soldiers, and the victors congratulate one another. Henry wakes from a brief nap to find that the enemy is again charging his regiment. Terror overtakes him this time and he leaps up and flees from the line. As he scampers across the landscape, he tells himself that he did the right thing, that his regiment could not have won, and that the men who remained to fight were fools. He passes a general on horseback and overhears the com-mander saying that the regiment has held back the enemy charge. Ashamed of his cowardice, Henry tries to convince himself that he was right to preserve his own life. He wanders through a forest glade in which he encounters the decaying corpse of a soldier. Shaken, he hur-ries away.

After a time, Henry joins a column of wounded soldiers winding down the road. He is deeply envious of these men, thinking that a wound is like "a red badge of courage"; visible proof of valorous behav-ior. He meets a tattered man who has been shot twice and who speaks proudly of the fact that his regiment did not flee. He repeatedly asks Henry where he is wounded, which makes Henry deeply uncomfortable and compels him to hurry away to a different part of the column. He meets a spectral soldier with a distant, numb look on his face. Henry eventually recognizes the man as a badly wounded Jim Conklin. Henry promises to take care of Jim, but Jim runs from the line into a small grove of bushes where Henry and the tattered man watch him die.

Henry and the tattered soldier wander through the woods. Henry hears the rumble of combat in the distance. The tattered soldier continues to ask Henry about his wound, even as his own health visibly worsens. At last, Henry is unable to bear the tattered man's questioning and abandons him to die in the forest.

Henry continues to wander until he finds himself close enough to the battlefield to be able to watch some of the fighting. He sees a blue regiment in retreat and attempts to stop the soldiers to find out what has happened. One of the fleeing men hits him on the head with a rifle, opening a bloody gash on Henry's head. Eventually, another soldier leads Henry to his regiment's camp, where Henry is reunited with his companions. His friend Wilson, believing that Henry has been shot, cares for him tenderly.

The next day, the regiment proceeds back to the battlefield. Henry fights like a lion. Thinking of Jim Conklin, he vents his rage against the enemy soldiers. His lieutenant says that with ten thousand Henrys, he could win the war in a week. Nevertheless, Henry and Wilson overhear an officer say that the soldiers of the 304th fight like "mule drivers." Insulted, they long to prove the man wrong. In an ensuing charge, the regiment's color bearer falls. Henry takes the flag and carries it proudly before the regiment. After the charge fails, the derisive officer tells the regiment's colonel that his men fight like "mud diggers," further infuriating Henry. Another soldier tells Henry and Wilson, to their gratification, that the colonel and lieutenant consider them the best fighters in the regiment.

The group is sent into more fighting, and Henry continues to carry the flag. The regiment charges a group of enemy soldiers fortified behind a fence, and, after a pitched battle, wins the fence. Wilson seizes the enemy flag and the regiment takes four prisoners. As he and the others march back to their position, Henry reflects on his experiences in the war. Though he revels in his recent success in battle, he feels deeply ashamed of his behavior the previous day, especially his abandonment of the tattered man. But after a moment, he puts his guilt behind him and realizes that he has come through "the red sickness" of battle. He is now able to look forward to peace, feeling a quiet, steady manhood within himself.

Henry Fleming—The novel's protagonist; a young soldier fighting for the Union army during the American Civil War. Initially, Henry stands untested in battle and questions his own courage. As the novel progresses, he encounters hard truths about the experience of war, confronting the universe's indifference to his existence and the insignificance of his own life. Often vain and holding extremely romantic notions about himself, Henry grapples with these lessons as he first runs from battle, then comes to thrive as a soldier in combat.

Jim Conklin—Henry's friend; a tall soldier hurt during the regiment's first battle. Jim soon dies from his wounds, and represents, in the early part of the novel, an important moral contrast to Henry.

Wilson—A loud private; Henry's friend in the regiment. Wilson and Henry grow close as they share the harsh experiences of war and gain a reputation as the regiment's best fighters. Wilson proves to be a more sympathetic version of Henry, though he does not seem to be troubled by Henry's tendency to endlessly scrutinize his own actions.

The tattered soldier—A twice-shot soldier whom Henry encounters in the column of wounded men. With his endless speculation about Henry's supposed wound, the tattered soldier functions as a nagging, painful conscience to Henry.

The lieutenant—Henry's commander in battle, a youthful officer who swears profusely during the fighting. As Henry gains recognition for doing brave deeds, he and the lieutenant develop sympathy for each other, often feeling that they must work together to motivate the rest of the men.

Henry's mother—Encountered only in a brief flashback, Henry's mother opposed his enlisting in the army. Though her advice is only briefly summarized in Henry's flashback, it contains several difficult themes with which Henry must grapple, including the insignificance of his life in the grand scheme of the world.

HENRY FLEMING

Throughout the novel, Crane refers to Henry as "the young soldier" and "the youth." Both the best and worst characteristics of Henry's youth mark him. Unlike the veteran soldiers whom he encounters during his first battle, Henry is not jaded. He believes, albeit naïvely, in traditional models of courage and honor, and romanticizes the image of dying in battle by invoking the Greek tradition of a dead soldier being laid upon his shield. On the other hand, because he is young, Henry has yet to experience enough to test these abstractions. As a result, his most passionate convictions are based on little else than fantasies, making him seem vain and self-centered.

Henry's reasons for wanting to win glory in battle are far from noble. The philosophical underpinnings of the war do not motivate him; neither does any deeply held, personal sense of right and wrong. Instead, Henry desires a reputation. He hopes that an impressive performance on the battlefield will immortalize him as a hero among men who, because of the domesticating effects of religion and education, rarely distinguish themselves so dramatically. Ironically, after fleeing from battle, Henry feels little guilt about invoking his own intelligence in order to justify his cowardice. He condemns the soldiers who stayed to fight as imbeciles who were not "wise enough to save themselves from the flurry of death." This is how he restores his fragile self-pride. When Henry returns to camp and lies about the nature of his wound, he doubts neither his manhood nor his right to behave as pompously as a veteran. Henry's lack of a true moral sense manifests itself in the emptiness of the honor and glory that he seeks. He feels no responsibility to earn these accolades. If others call him a hero, he believes he is one.

When Henry finally faces battle, however, he feels a "temporary but sublime absence of selfishness." A great change occurs within him: as he fights, he loses his sense of self. No longer is he interested in winning the praise and attention of other men; instead, he allows himself to disappear into the commotion and become one component of a great fighting machine. As Henry finds himself deeply immersed in battle, the importance of winning a name for himself fades with the gun smoke, for "it was difficult to think of reputation when others were thinking of skins." It is ironic, then, that Henry establishes his reputation at these very moments. Officers who witness his fierce fighting regard him as one of the regiment's best. Henry does not cheat his way to the honor that he so desperately craves when the novel opens; instead, he *earns* it. This marks a tremendous growth in Henry's character. He learns to reflect on his mistakes, such as his earlier retreat, without defensiveness or bravado, and abandons the hope of blustery heroism for a quieter, but more satisfying, understanding of what it means to be a man.

JIM CONKLIN

Jim contrasts sharply with Henry in the opening pages of the novel. When Henry asks Jim if he would flee from battle, Jim's answer—that he would run if other soldiers ran, fight if they fought—establishes him as a pragmatist. He is strong and self-reliant, and does not romanticize war or its supposed glories in the manner that Henry does. Unlike Wilson, whose loud complaints characterize his early appearances, Jim marches through his days efficiently and with few grievances. He informs Henry that he can unburden himself of his unnecessary munitions, declaring, "You can now eat and shoot . . . That's all you want to do."

Jim has little patience for the kind of loud, knee-jerk criticism or vague abstraction that distracts Wilson and Henry. He prefers to do what duty requires of him and finds a quiet, simple pleasure in doing so. He silences Wilson and Henry from discussing the qualifications of their commanding officers while they are eating because he "could not rage in fierce argument in the presence of such sandwiches."

Jim's quiet demeanor persists even as he dies. He does not indulge in a protracted death scene, curse his fate, or philosophize about the cruelties and injustices of war. Instead, he brushes Henry and his offers of comfort aside. He seeks to die alone, and those present notice "a curious and profound dignity in the firm lines of his awful face." The solemn poise with which Jim dies puzzles Henry, who wants to rail loudly at the universe. In death, as in life, Jim possesses the rare, self-assured goodness of a man who knows and fulfills his responsibilities.

WILSON

Whereas Jim Conklin's character remains notably steady throughout the novel, Wilson undergoes a dramatic change. Wilson is initially loud, opinionated, and naïve. For the first half of the book, Crane refers to him almost exclusively as "the loud soldier." Wilson indignantly assures Henry that if battle occurs, he will certainly fight in it: "I said I was going to do my share of the fighting—that's what I said. And I am, too. Who are you anyhow? You talk as if you thought you was Napoleon Bonaparte." Shortly thereafter, he approaches Henry again. Certain that he is about to meet his doom, he gives the youth a yellow envelope to deliver to his family should he die in battle. This erratic shift from obnoxious bravado to naked vulnerability demonstrates Wilson's immaturity. Like Henry, he is initially little more than a youth trying desperately to assure himself of his manhood.

Wilson's transformation becomes clear relatively quickly. After disappearing into battle, he resurfaces to take care of Henry with all of the bustling of an "amateur nurse" upon Henry's return to camp. He further displays his generosity by insisting that Henry take his blanket. Upon waking the next day, Henry notes the change in his friend: "He was no more a loud young soldier. There was now about him a fine reliance. He showed a quiet belief in his purpose and his abilities."

Wilson's attitude toward the envelope which he earlier entrusted to Henry further demonstrates the maturation that he has undergone. Though ashamed of his earlier display of fear, he asks Henry for the envelope back—he is no longer interested in his reputation or in the amount of sheer bravery that his comrades associate with his name, two issues that ponderously plague Henry. Instead, Wilson seems to have "climbed a peak of wisdom from which he could perceive himself as a very wee thing."

This transformation furthers one of the novel's explorations, showing plainly what happens when one realizes the relative insignificance of his or her life—an awareness that Henry seems to have gained by the novel's end. Furthermore, the development of Wilson's character contributes to the noise/silence motif. Through the sounds of battle, endless gossip, and empty bragging of the soldiers, noise comes to be associated with youth, vanity, and struggle. Toward the end of the novel, these sounds give way to a peace and quiet that suggest the eventuality of the progression past youthful struggle to the more reflective musings of manhood.

THEMES

Themes are the fundamental and often universal ideas explored in a literary work.

Courage

Given the novel's title, it is no surprise that courage—defining it, desiring it, and, ultimately, achieving it—is the most salient element of the narrative. As the novel opens, Henry's understanding of courage is traditional and romantic. He assumes that, like a war hero of ancient Greece, he will return from battle either *with* his shield or *on* it. Henry's understanding of courage has more to do with the praise of his peers than any internal measure of his bravery. Within the novel's first chapter, Henry recalls his mother's advice, which runs counter to his own notions. She cares little whether Henry earns himself a praiseworthy name; instead, she instructs him to meet his responsibilities honestly and squarely, even if it means sacrificing his own life.

The gap that exists between Henry's definition of courage and the alternative that his mother suggests fluctuates throughout *The Red Badge of Courage,* sometimes narrowing (when Henry fights well in his first battle) and sometimes growing wider (when he abandons the tattered soldier). At the end of the novel, as the mature Henry marches victoriously from battle, a more subtle and complex understanding of courage emerges: it is not simply a function of other people's opinions, but it does incorporate egocentric concerns such as a soldier's regard for his reputation.

Manhood

Throughout the novel, Henry struggles to preserve his manhood, his understanding of which parallels his understanding of courage. At first, he relies on very traditional, even clichéd, notions. He laments that education and religion have tamed men of their natural savagery and made them so pale and domestic that there remain few ways for a man to distinguish himself other than on the battlefield. Having this opportunity makes Henry feel grateful to be participating in the war. As he makes his way from one skirmish to the next, he becomes more and more convinced that his accumulated experiences will earn him the praise of women and the envy of men; he will be a hero, a *real* man, in their eyes. These early conceptions of manhood are simplistic, romantic, adolescent fantasies.

Jim Conklin and Wilson stand as symbols of a more human kind of manhood. They are self-assured without being braggarts and are ultimately able to own up to their faults and shortcomings. Wilson, who begins the novel as an obnoxiously loud soldier, later exposes his own fear and vulnerability when he asks Henry to deliver a yellow envelope to his family should he die in battle. In realizing the relative insignificance of his own life, Wilson frees himself from the chains that bind Henry, becoming a man of "quiet belief in his purposes and abilities." By the novel's end, Henry makes a bold step in the same direction, learning that the measure of one's manhood lies more in the complex ways in which one negotiates one's mistakes and responsibilities than in one's conduct on the battlefield.

Self-Preservation

An anxious desire for self-preservation influences Henry throughout the novel. When a pinecone that he throws after fleeing from battle makes a squirrel scurry, he believes that he has stumbled upon a universal truth: each being will do whatever it takes, including running from danger, in order to preserve itself. Henry gets much mileage out of this revelation, as he uses it to justify his impulse to retreat from the battlefield. His conceits—namely that the good of the army and, by extension, the world, requires his survival—drive him to behave abominably. He not only runs from battle, but also abandons the tattered soldier, though he knows that the soldier is almost certain to die if he does not receive assistance. Soon after his encounter with the squirrel, Henry discovers the corpse of a soldier. This sets in motion Henry's realization that the world is largely indifferent to his life and the questions that preoccupy him. Courage and honor endow a man with a belief in the worth of preserving the lives of others, but the pervasiveness of death on the battlefield compels Henry to question the importance of these qualities. This weighing of values begs consideration of the connection between the survival instinct and vanity.

The Universe's Disregard for Human Life

Henry's realization that the natural world spins on regardless of the manner in which men live and die is perhaps the most difficult lesson that Henry learns as a soldier. It disabuses him of his naïve, inexperienced beliefs regarding courage and manhood. Shortly after his encounter with the squirrel in the woods, Henry stumbles upon a dead soldier, whose rotting body serves as a powerful reminder of the universe's indifference to human life. As the drama of the war rages on around him, Henry continues to occupy his mind with questions concerning the nature of courage and honor and the possibilities of gaining glory. Death, he assumes, would stop this drama cold. Yet, when he encounters the corpse, he finds that death is nothing more than an integral and unremarkable part of nature. As he reflects at the end of the novel: "He had been to touch the great death, and found that, after all, it was but the great death."

Together, Henry's encounters with the squirrel and the corpse form one of the most important passages in the novel, for it is here that Crane establishes the formidable opposing forces in Henry's mind: the vain belief that human life deserves such distinctions as courage and honor, and the stark realization that, regardless of such distinctions, all human life meets the same end.

MOTIFS

Motifs are recurring structures, contrasts, or literary devices that can help to develop and inform the text's major themes.

Noise and Silence

Great and terrible sounds saturate much of the novel. The book opens with soldiers chattering, gossiping, and arguing about when and if they will see action on the battlefield. Soon enough, the pop of gunfire and exploding artillery drown out their conversations. The reader comes to associate these sounds with boys, battle—both physical and mental—

and bravado. Wilson, who often airs his opinions indignantly, embodies these associations early in the novel when Crane refers to him almost exclusively as "the loud soldier." The transformation of Wilson and Henry into men of quiet resolve marks a process of maturation, wherein a peaceful disposition wins out over an unquiet one and the security of feeling courage internally silences the need for public recognition.

Youth and Maturity

Although the novel spans no more than a few weeks, the reader witnesses a profound change in the characters of both Henry and Wilson. Though these men do not grow considerably older during the course of the narrative, one can best describe the psychological development that the novel charts for them as the passage from youth into maturity. Innocence gives way to experience, and the unfounded beliefs of boys make way for the quietly assured, bedrock convictions of men.

SYMBOLS

Symbols are objects, characters, figures, or colors used to represent abstract ideas or concepts.

The Dead Soldier

In writing *The Red Badge of Courage,* Crane tried to render battle, and the lives of common soldiers, as authentically as possible. Accordingly, a realistic, almost journalistic style of writing dominates the narrative, leaving little room for the development of an overt, more literary system of symbols. However, there are a few noteworthy symbols in the novel. One of these is the dead soldier, who represents the insignificance of mortal concerns. Henry encounters the corpse, decaying and covered by ants, at a crucial moment: he has just reassured himself that he was right to flee battle and that the welfare of the army depends upon soldiers being wise enough to preserve themselves. Then the dead soldier, whose anonymity strips him of any public recognition of courage and glory (regardless of whether or not he deserved them), forces Henry to begin to question himself and the values by which he measures his actions.

CHAPTER I

Summary

> *Whatever he had learned of himself was here of no avail. He was an unknown quantity.*

On a cold, foggy morning, an army wakes on the banks of a river. A tall soldier named Jim Conklin begins his day by washing his shirt, and rushes back to camp to report a rumor he has overheard: the regiment will move into battle the next day. As the men in this particular squad have yet to face any military action, Jim's words provoke much excitement and debate. One private loudly declares Conklin a liar, and a corporal complains that he would not have made costly renovations to his house if he had known he would be called to leave it. Henry Fleming, a young private, listens attentively to the arguments, then retreats to his bunk to collect his thoughts.

Having dreamed of the glory and valor of battle since childhood, Henry cannot believe that he may find himself in the heat of combat the very next day. He wonders if soldiers in his regiment can possibly achieve the same glory that the ancient Greek war heroes did. He believes that religion, education, and common household concerns have tamed men, sapping them of "the throat-grappling instinct," but that, in battle, they can still prove themselves worthy. In fact, the conviction that battle may be the *only* way for a man to distinguish himself prompted Henry to enlist in the first place. He remembers how his mother discouraged this course of action, how she refused to share in his romantic ideas of dying a celebrated war hero. He thinks of her parting advice to him: never to do anything he would feel ashamed to tell her. She encourages him to do the right thing and not to shirk his duties for the sake of returning home alive to care for her; she assures him that she will carry on whether or not he returns.

Henry remembers his journey to Washington, where the regiment assembled and enjoyed abundance of food, the friendly smiles of girls, and the assurances of men. There, Henry felt as if he had become a hero. The months that followed his enlistment, however, were monotonous and static. The daily grind of camp life has forced Henry to abandon thoughts of glory. He struggles, instead, to preserve his own personal well-being. Given his discomfort, Henry wonders if he will be capable of thriving in battle. With rumors of a march into a fierce skirmish the following day, Henry realizes that his character has gone untested up until this point in his life. He wonders if he has the fortitude to endure battle, or if cowardice will make him flee. When Jim returns to the tent, Henry asks him if he would ever consider running from battle. Jim answers that he would likely follow the cues of the men surrounding him, fighting when they fought, running when they ran. Henry feels relieved that he is not alone in questioning his own courage.

Analysis

Readers at the end of the nineteenth century, for many of whom the American Civil War was a recent memory, were accustomed to reading about the Civil War as a grand, morally charged clash of ideals. Writers such as Frederick Douglass, Abraham Lincoln, and Walt Whitman treated the conflict—especially the fight to abolish slavery—as a means of fulfilling the American dream and promise of freedom. Crane, however, skirts the moral terrain of the war by focusing instead on the day-to-day reality that an untested regiment of soldiers faces. If a clear-cut dividing line can be drawn between the concerns of the warring North and South, Crane does little to honor it. He does not introduce a band of righteous, well-fitted soldiers who represent all that is good and glorious. Instead, he depicts a group of soldiers who are, for the most part, utterly amateur. They have never fought, they hold their commanding officers in contempt, and they have no sense of the glory commonly associated with military service. In short, Crane places the reader squarely in the sphere of realism, which attempts to portray life as it is, rather than allegory, which uses symbolism to convey meaning.

Whereas the early nineteenth century brought forth writers who sought to escape or transcend reality, and who often wrote in a flowery style, writers in the latter part of the century, according to William Dean

Howells, insisted on "nothing more and nothing less than the truthful treatment of materials." Although powerful and evocative, Crane's descriptions of the army, life in the camp, and the natural surroundings are stripped of unnecessarily ornamental language. Crane records both the daily life of the soldiers and Henry's complex inner musings in clear, direct, unadorned prose:

> The youth was in a little trance of astonishment. So they were at last going to fight. On the morrow, perhaps, there would be a battle, and he would be in it. For a time he was obliged to labor to make himself believe. He could not accept with assurance an omen that he was about to mingle in one of those great affairs of the earth.

The main battle of *The Red Badge of Courage* is the psychological one that takes place in Henry's head. From the moment he is introduced, Henry struggles to reconcile the fanciful narratives of larger-than-life heroes emerging from bloody but valorous battles with the much plainer, much less glorified existence of life in the 304th Regiment. When he learns that he may soon be placed on the battlefront, he begins to weigh the war that he imagined against the war in which he actually finds himself. He wonders if he, like the heroes of Ancient Greece before him, will return from battle "with his shield or on it."

The novel focuses on Henry's concern about dying without recognition versus achieving public glory. Within the first few pages, Henry appears vain and self-centered. His idea of glory falls short of the Homeric heroes whom he praises, for he lacks their requisite sense of duty. He does not consider earning or proving himself worthy of public recognition nearly as important as the recognition itself. So long as he is met by smiling girls and appreciative men, he is content to think of himself as a hero. However, as the possibility of battle draws closer, and Henry begins to question whether he deserves the accolades he desires, both Henry and the reader are forced to question traditional understandings of such abstract concepts as glory, cowardice and, of course, courage.

Chapters II–IV

Summary

Chapter II

The next morning, the soldiers learn that Jim was mistaken: the army does not move. Henry continues to worry about his courage, and watches his comrades closely for any sign that they share his self-doubt. One day, the army is given orders and begins to march. While marching, the soldiers continue to debate when and if they will see battle. Henry keeps to himself, too preoccupied with his own speculations to join the other men. The regiment enjoys itself, and is wildly amused when a fat soldier attempts to steal a horse but the young girl who owns it stops him. At night, the men set up camp, and Henry, feeling "vast pity for himself," asks Wilson if he can imagine himself running from battle. Wilson loudly and indignantly claims that he would do his part in a battle, and leaves Henry feeling even more alone.

Chapter III

The next night finds the increasingly exhausted soldiers marching through a dark forest. Henry worries that the enemy might appear at any moment. When the enemy fails to materialize, Henry returns to thinking that his regiment is nothing more than a "blue demonstration." One morning, however, Jim shakes Henry awake. They hear the crack of distant gunfire, and the regiment begins to run. Boxed in by his fellow soldiers as the officers goad them toward the battle, Henry realizes that even if he wanted to run, the throng of surrounding soldiers would trample him. Pressed forward, the regiment parts to move around the body of a dead soldier. As he passes the corpse, Henry grows increasingly vulnerable, and curses the commanding officers who, it seems, are leading them to certain death.

The men stop several times, many of them using branches and stones to build protective trenches which they must invariably abandon as the march drives them forward. The more the regiment moves, the faster the soldiers' morale wanes. They gradually begin to think that their leaders are incompetent and indecisive. As the fighting draws closer and the sound of gunfire grows louder, Wilson tells Henry that he believes he will die in the battle. He gives Henry a yellow envelope and asks him to deliver it to his family should he not make it home.

Chapter IV

The regiment stops in a grove with the chaos of battle raging around them. The regiment's lieutenant is shot in the hand. The soldiers of the 304th take their place on the line, and veteran soldiers who mock their inexperience surround them. As a group of enemy soldiers thunders toward them, Henry and his regiment load their weapons and prepare to engage. Miserably, Henry remains convinced that when he has to confront the worst that war has to offer, he might distinguish himself not by how bravely he fights, but by how quickly he runs away.

Analysis

The self-doubt awakened in Henry in Chapter I continues to plague him as he draws closer to battle in Chapter II. He oscillates between grand, dramatic fantasies of the "traditional courage" that leads to glory in the field and an innocent belief that the army is never going to fight, that his regiment, rendered impotent by Christian education, constitutes merely a "blue demonstration." Henry's experiences eventually shatter these preconceptions. His development into a man who understands that courage, duty, and manhood are complicated and sometimes compromised is the most compelling aspect of *The Red Badge of Courage*.

Even at this early stage, there are excellent opportunities to scrutinize Henry's conflicted character. He is incredibly vain, he obsesses over his own feelings, and seems unwilling to differentiate between moral behavior and behavior that simply wins him the envy and praise of others. In other words, he is less concerned with *duty* than with *glory*. He fears being exposed as a coward not because cowardice marks a shirking of his responsibilities as a soldier, but because such exposure would deny him an illustrious reputation. After all, Henry's desire for a noble name prompts his enlistment in the first place—he feels little obligation to *earn* the title of hero. Rather, the "lavish expenditure" of food, smiles, and compliments that he meets on the way to Washington proves to be enough to make him believe that he deserves such rewards.

As the novel progresses, Henry comes to the painful realization of his own insignificance in the grand scheme of the universe—as his mother tells him in Chapter I, he is "jest one little feller amongst a hull lot of others." When the marching troops come across a corpse, Henry feels "the impulse of the living to try to read in dead eyes the answer to the Question." "The Question" is never articulated, but the answer, which Henry moves closer and closer to learning, has much to do with understanding the modest and fragile proportions of one's life and the meaning of honor. Crane uses passing moments such as Henry's memory of his mother's advice and this first encounter with a dead soldier to plant some of the novel's larger ideas in the reader's mind. The narrative's major thematic concerns, such as the irresolvable tensions between self-preservation and the impetus to behave honorably, begin to be defined.

CHAPTERS V–VII

Summary

Chapter V

He suddenly lost concern for himself . . . He was welded into a common personality which was dominated by a single desire.

After a tense wait, the enemy soldiers attack and Henry's regiment begins to fire upon them. The captain stands behind Henry's regiment shouting instructions. As he faces the threat of the advancing troops, Henry loses his sense of being a lone, miserable outcast and begins to conceive of himself as a single cog in a machine. The battle overshadows his individuality by making him one with his fellow soldiers, just as the instinct to fight overcomes his timid, intellectual musings. The battle rages and Henry fires and reloads, fires and reloads, in a continuing, automatic rhythm. A "red rage" overtakes the men, who chant a "wild, barbaric song" as they fight. The lieutenant beats a soldier who tries to retreat from the frontline. The captain is shot and collapses. At last, the enemy soldiers begin to retreat. Henry's regiment lets out a cheer and the survivors heartily congratulate one another. Henry looks around; seeing the sun on the treetops and the bright blue sky, he is surprised that Nature keeps on going, with no regard for the bloody events of the field.

. . . upon his face there was an astonished and sorrowful look, as if he thought some friend had done him an ill turn.

Chapter VI

A short while later, Henry awakes and feels delighted with himself. He thinks he has survived the horror of battle and proved his courage. He and the other members of the regiment draw themselves up proudly and praise one another's fortitude and valor, shaking hands in an ecstasy of mutual self-satisfaction. Suddenly, someone cries out that the enemy forces have renewed the charge. The men groan dejectedly and prepare to repel the attack. This time, Henry does not feel as though he is part of a machine. He thinks that the enemy soldiers must be awe-inspiring men to have such persistence, and he panics. One by one, soldiers from Henry's regiment begin to jump up and flee from the line, and after a moment, Henry too runs away.

Henry flees from the battlefield, convinced that at any moment, the charging enemy horde will burst out of the forest and overrun him. He darts past a battery of gunmen, pitying them their position in the path of the enemy. He skulks past a general giving orders to his staff from atop a horse, and feels the desire to throttle the general for his incompetent handling of the battle. To his shock, he overhears the general declare that the enemy has been held back.

Chapter VII

Henry feels a sudden resentment toward those in his regiment who did not run but rather defeated the enemy without him; he feels betrayed by their stupidity. To assuage his own feelings of guilt and incompetence, he assures himself that any thinking man would have realized that the best interest of the army lay in each soldier's own self-preservation. Consumed by these rationalizations, he plunges into the woods. Now far from the battle, Henry feels comforted by nature. He tosses a pinecone at a squirrel, and the squirrel scampers into a tree. Henry considers this sequence proof that fleeing from danger is a natural, universal tendency. He stumbles into a forest grove whose high ceiling of leaves makes it resemble a chapel. There he discovers the dead body of a soldier in a tattered blue uniform much like Henry's. Ants swarm over the corpse's face. Henry stares in shock for a moment and then runs from the glade, half expecting the corpse to cry out after him.

Analysis

Henry's loss of individuality in the heat of battle marks his first experience with the nature of war and its powerful effect upon the mind. He realizes the emptiness of his belief that glory is bestowed almost automatically upon individuals who meet battle squarely and fiercely when he observes "a singular absence of heroic poses." Rather, he loses all sense of self and fights with his fellow soldiers as though all were components of a single machine. This sense of commonality allows Henry's recognition of the greater good of the regiment to prevail over his selfish desire to avoid death.

The cheerful, self-congratulatory mood following the battle initiates a cycle that repeats itself throughout the novel: when the soldiers prevail, they feel confident and satisfied until forced to fight again, at which point their fearfulness returns; when they lose, they feel dejected and unsure of themselves until they receive a chance to fight again and redeem themselves. As the novel progresses, however, the regiment gradually hardens and shares an increasingly grimmer and more controlled attitude toward combat, keeping their emotions in check until the fighting is really over. In this way, the regiment of inexperienced soldiers matures into a veteran unit.

Henry's second experience of battle further complicates his assumptions about war, as he unexpectedly panics and flees. The egotistic nature of Henry's mind (which, because it is the only mind in the novel to which the reader has access, represents every soldier's mind) reveals itself as Henry works desperately to restore his own self-confidence by making irrational justifications. These passages, which Crane wrote in his most sardonic and detached voice, are often quite comic. For example, when Henry imagines that "he had been wronged" by the regiment's success in the battle after his flight, and when he condemns the victorious soldiers for being too stupid to follow him. This criticism is ironic, given Henry's belief that fine minds keep men from fighting bravely in battle. The network of naïve assumptions and grandiose self-delusions in Henry's mind supports him as he struggles to restore his own sense of importance.

This struggle renders Henry far more complex than a merely vain and self-absorbed character. The briefest glimpse of war has challenged Henry's understanding of his own significance and has shaken the foundations of his deepest beliefs: his understanding of courage, honor, and manhood. This threat to Henry's faith in his own special and deserving nature opens the way for the most important thematic exploration in the novel: his acknowledgment that the universe does not care whether he lives or dies. Henry realizes that just as the world spins around the anonymous soldier's dead body, so will it spin around his. This important insight about the relative inconsequentiality of a given life finds representation throughout these three chapters, as in the sun's gleaming on the trees after the first battle, surprising Henry that "nature had gone tranquilly on with her golden process in the midst of so much devilment."

The corpse is one of the most important metaphors in the early part of the novel, symbolizing both the finality of death and the indifference of nature to the elimination of a human consciousness. Rooted, immobile, and swarming with ants, the corpse is an undeniable part of the scenery. No amount of mediation on courage or investigation into whether the dead soldier lived honorably will change the essential, inescapable fact of his death—neither his deeds nor his reputation matter. The sight of the dead soldier undoes the comfortable moral assumption that the squirrel's flight from danger affords Henry, and shows him that his logic has been too simple: there may be no compass of right and wrong to which he might cling in this situation, no overriding moral truth fundamental to the nature of the universe. Henry learns that death may simply be death, and the universe may not care about his fear of it.

CHAPTERS VIII–X

Summary

Chapter VIII

Stomping through the forest, Henry hears "the crimson roar" of battle. Hoping to get a closer look, he heads toward it. He comes upon a column of wounded men stumbling along a road, and notices one spectral soldier with a vacant gaze. Henry joins the column and a soldier with a bloody head and a dangling arm begins to talk to him. Henry tries to avoid this tattered man, but the wounded soldier continues talking about the courage and fortitude of the army, exuding pride that his regiment did not flee from the fighting. He asks Henry where he has been wounded, and Henry hurries away in a panic.

Chapter IX

Henry falls back in the procession to avoid the tattered man. As he observes the wounded soldiers around him, he becomes envious of their injuries; he considers a wound proof of valor—a "red badge of courage"—and wishes that he had one. He walks by the spectral soldier that he noticed earlier, a gray man staring blankly into "the unknown." Henry suddenly realizes the man's identity and cries out: "Gawd! Jim Conklin!" Jim greets Henry wearily and asks where he has been, telling him, "I got shot."

Jim adds that he is afraid of falling down and being run over by the artillery wagons. Henry promises to take care of him. Jim seems reassured, but soon orders Henry to leave him alone and not touch him. Baffled, Henry tries to lead Jim into the fields, where the artillery wagons will not frighten him, but Jim musters the strength to run away toward a small clump of bushes. Henry and the tattered man follow after him, watching in horror as Jim convulses, collapses, and dies. The flap of Jim's blue jacket falls away from his body, and Henry sees that his side looks "as if it had been chewed by wolves." Consumed with rage at his friend's death, Henry clenches his fist and shakes it angrily in the direction of the battlefield.

Chapter X

The tattered man marvels at the strength that Jim mustered before death, wondering how he managed to run when his injury should have rendered him unable to walk. Henry and the tattered man move away from the corpse. The tattered man says that he is feeling "pretty damn' bad," and Henry worries that he is about to witness another death. The tattered man says, however, that he is not about to die—he has children who need him to survive. He mistakes Henry for his friend Tom Jamison and tells him that he also looks weak, and that he should have his wound looked at. He adds that he once saw a man shot in the head so that the man did not realize he was hurt until he was already dead.

Tormented, Henry leaves the tattered man behind. As he stalks away, the tattered man, who Henry knows will almost certainly die if abandoned, seems to lose his focus, and begins crying out to Henry. Driven to distraction by the tattered man's questions about his wound, Henry cannot bear the thought of anyone discovering "his crime."

Analysis

The encounters with Jim and the tattered man force Henry to reconcile fantasy with reality. He views the wounded soldiers as heroic and enviable, but watches two of them die. Henry is deeply ashamed of his own cowardice in running from battle, and longs for a wound to validate his nerve. But the soldiers who acted as he wishes he could have—one of them his childhood friend Jim Conklin—both die of their wounds. The apparent necessity of navigating this conflict between life and honor troubles Henry greatly.

Nowhere in the novel is the tension between the human instinct of self-preservation and the impetus toward moral behavior stronger or more upsetting to Henry. Though he anxiously wishes to act bravely to earn the praise and envy of others, he is deeply afraid to die. The pathetic fates of the tattered man and Jim arouse these conflicting emotions in Henry, causing him to experience an almost unbearable self-doubt. He modifies the positive connection between battle wound and courage into an inverse correlation between battle wound and shame: since he has not been injured, he feels that his disgrace is visible to everyone around him. Too immature to confront his insecurities, Henry evades them by rashly abandoning the dying, tattered man, whose battle wound underscores the courage that Henry lacks.

Henry's various experiences with nature's indifference to human concerns further complicate his outlook by removing his sense of moral absolutes: if the universe has no regard for human concerns, then human moral conventions do not reflect a definitive, natural spectrum of right and wrong. Henry comes to believe that human beings are not inherently moral animals; rather, they have simply constructed an arbitrary and inflexible system of morality that often runs counter to their own instincts. In contrast, nature's definitive, nonarbitrary judgments of right and wrong change with, and are dependent on, the human value of self-preservation.

In this environment the idea of a wound appeals immensely to the troubled, young Henry. While it may seem ironic that an individual who fears danger would long for an injury, Henry considers a wound irrefutable proof of the moral position he so desperately seeks, a symbol not only of courage but also of an entire value system that nature ignores.

CHAPTERS XI–XII

Summary

Chapter XI

The noise of battle grows into a "furnace roar" and Henry comes upon a line of soldiers and wagons inching down the road. He watches a column of infantry hurrying to reach the battle and senses that he is "regarding a procession of chosen beings." The enthusiastic soldiers increase Henry's feelings of wretchedness, underscoring, he believes, his own inadequacy. He feels a brief rush of violent enthusiasm and nearly starts out for the battlefield himself, but quickly talks himself out of it: he has no rifle, he is hungry and thirsty, and his body is sore and aching. He hovers near the battlefield, though, hoping to get to see who is winning. He thinks that if his side loses, it will partially justify his actions and prove the almost prophetic powers of perception that enabled him to predict this defeat. He alleviates his guilt for wishing his comrades ill by reflecting that his army has overcome every defeat it has faced in the past. Still, he feels deeply guilty and brands himself a terrible villain and "the most unutterably selfish man in existence."

Henry does not believe that the soldiers in blue can possibly lose the battle. He therefore resolves to come up with a story to justify his actions to his fellow soldiers when they return to camp, so that they will not scorn him when he rejoins them. He is unable to concoct a sufficient excuse, however, and fears that he is doomed to bear the contempt of his comrades and that his name will become slang for coward.

Chapter XII

Henry finally gets a look at the battlefield and sees the enemy forces swallowing the column of infantrymen he envied earlier. The blue line breaks and the blue soldiers retreat. Soon, they rush toward him. Desperate and overwhelmed by the sights and sounds of warfare, Henry clutches a fleeing man's arm and tries to ask him what went wrong. The frenzied man shouts at Henry to let him go and, when Henry does not comply, slams the butt of his rifle into Henry's head. Bloodied, Henry collapses and tries to stumble out of the crowd of retreating men. He meets a cheerful stranger who talks to him about the battle and helps him to find his own regiment. As the stranger points Henry to his regiment's campfire and disappears into the forest, Henry realizes that he never once saw the man's face.

Analysis

These transitional chapters carry Henry from the depth of his greatest despair to his reunion with his regiment. As noted previously, part of Henry's longing for a wound stems from the fact that he considers a wound to be undeniable proof of courage in battle. Henry's wounding is ironic as it in no way involves courageous behavior on his part. Because it happens as a result of a desperate misunderstanding with a comrade and would not have occurred had Henry been in battle, this wounding is a disgrace rather than a source of pride. Whereas Henry sought a wound as an emblem of courage, his actual wound is an emblem of shame.

Henry's view of right and wrong is still at least partially rooted in his weighty consideration of the opinions of his peers: he does not feel shame for failing to honor the cause of the Union against the Confederacy, but because he believes his friends will jeer at him. Henry may seem despicable at such moments—Crane frequently holds him up for criticism—but it is important to remember that Henry's folly could well be anyone's. Henry is beset by common, human emotions, making him an object of empathy.

Crane continues to divest both the Union and Confederate armies of any moral qualities or idealistic associations: they do not represent ideas, cultures, or beliefs in this novel; they are simply two colors on a battlefield. These armies are never referred to by name—Henry Fleming does not fight for the Union army; he fights for the "blue" army. In fact, Henry is almost never even called by his name; he is usually referred to as "the youth" or "the young soldier," just as Wilson is called "the loud soldier." The elimination of proper names has multiple functions. First, it brings the story, concerned from the outset with larger-than-life notions of courage and honor, down to a more earthly level. These soldiers are common men leading common lives, which ultimately forces the reader to reconsider those traditionally lofty ideals. Second, anonymity lends the narrative a sense of universality, as the reader can imagine any soldier in any war facing the quandaries that plague Henry. In this manner, Crane broadens the novel's scope far beyond the single "Episode of the American Civil War" that its subtitle suggests.

Perhaps the strangest feature of these two chapters is the unnamed and faceless "cheerful soldier" who escorts Henry back to his camp. This character has an almost supernatural quality about him, and is the subject of numerous and colorful interpretations: some maintain that he is Jim Conklin's ghost, while others believe he represents Jesus Christ. In all probability, Crane's commitment to realism would have precluded an interpretation that makes the cheerful soldier a supernatural or divine being; instead, he seems simply one more bewildering element in the incomprehensible realm of battle.

CHAPTERS XIII–XV

Summary

Chapter XIII
Terrified that his fellow soldiers will revile him for fleeing from the battle, Henry totters toward the fire. He navigates his way past the bodies of his sleeping comrades with great difficulty. Suddenly a loud voice instructs him to halt. Henry recognizes Wilson standing guard. He informs Wilson that he has been shot in the head after being separated from the regiment and fighting with another group. His friend immediately turns him over to the corporal. The corporal examines him and decides that Henry has been grazed by a shell, which has left little more than a lump: "jest as if some feller had lammed yeh on th' head with a club." Wearily, Henry watches the camp until Wilson returns with a canteen of coffee. He nurses Henry, tending to his head with a wet cloth and giving him his blanket for the night. Grateful and dazed, Henry drifts off to sleep.

Chapter XIV

Henry wakes in the gray, misty dawn, feeling as though he has been "asleep for a thousand years." In the distance he hears the roar of fighting which rumbles around him with a "deadly persistency." Looking around at his sleeping comrades, Henry believes for a moment that he is surrounded by dead men and cries out in anguish. When the bugle blows, however, the men get up slowly. Wilson asks Henry how he feels as he tends to his head. "Pretty bad," Henry replies. As Wilson tends to Henry, Henry notices a change in his friend: he is no longer the loud soldier, that sensitive and prickly youth obsessed with his own sense of valor. Instead, he seems to have acquired a quiet, but remarkable, confidence. The two men discuss the battle, and Henry reports that Jim Conklin is dead. A group of soldiers exchanges harsh words near Henry and Wilson, nearly coming to blows. Wilson intervenes, keeps the peace, and returns to Henry. He says that the regiment lost more than half of its men the day before, but that many of them have since returned—they scattered in the woods, he reports, and fought with other regiments, just like Henry.

Chapter XV

> *He had performed his mistakes in the dark, so he was still a man.*

Henry remembers the yellow envelope that Wilson had asked to be delivered to his family upon his death. He is about to remind Wilson of it, but thinks better of this at the last moment. He believes that having the envelope—an emblem of Wilson's past vulnerability—will enable him to deflect any unpleasant questions Wilson might ask about Henry's activities during the previous day. For Henry, the envelope becomes an insurance policy against being caught in a lie, and his self-assurance is restored. He does not worry about the battles ahead of him, thinking that he is "doomed to greatness" and cannot be killed. He feels scorn for his comrades who ran from the battle the previous day, thinking that they fled more wildly than was necessary, while he himself "fled with discretion and dignity."

Wilson interrupts Henry's reverie by asking him for the envelope back. Henry returns it, and Wilson seems deeply embarrassed. Henry feels sorry for his friend and immensely superior to him; he imagines telling his mother and a young lady from his hometown stories of the war, and thinks that his tales will shatter their feeble preconceptions of heroism and combat.

Analysis

In preparing Henry for his next experience in battle, these three chapters focus almost entirely on his vanity, hypocrisy, and unfounded sense of superiority, which escalate by Chapter XV to an almost unbearable degree. As the narrative progresses, Henry allows the opinions of his peers to determine not only his sense of moral behavior, but also his very sense of truth. He feels no guilt upon discovering that his shameful injury can pass as a respect-inspiring, combat-inflicted wound. Further, even though he ran while Wilson fought, Henry feels superior to his friend when he remembers the yellow envelope, which he considers concrete proof of Wilson's cowardice. Without such proof to mark his own downfall, and with the validation of his wound as a testament to his alleged courage, Henry feels invincible: "He had performed his mistakes in the dark, so he was still a man." Though his main experience of war so far has been running from it, Henry demonstrates his stomach-turning vanity by imagining that he will soon regale the women in his life with his shocking and moving stories of battle.

Through such developments, Crane explores Henry's nearly limitless powers of self-delusion. In his desperate need to rebuild his shattered sense of importance, Henry blocks the coming battle out of his mind, content instead to rest upon his unearned laurels. Though he has yet to prove himself, Henry believes that he is destined to do great deeds. He is certain that fate, God, or the universe—the utter indifference of which has so recently shocked him—will keep him alive and thriving. Crane uses these passages to reveal the complex subtleties of man's instinctual impulse to survive, linking it to less excusable behaviors induced by self-deception and vanity.

Throughout *The Red Badge of Courage,* vanity and self-deception prove to be the mind's most successful strategy for coping with the extraordinary fragility and insignificance of human life. If not for self-delusion, the dangers one faces would drive one mad; if not for vanity, one's own unimportance would drive one to despair. Part of the instinct to survive hinges on the individual's belief in the importance of his own survival, the preciousness of his life. As a result of fleeing the dangers of war and the despair that follows them, Henry has come face to face with his own insignificance, and reacts in the only way available to him. To maintain control over his fears, he lies to those around him and then convinces himself that whatever they believe — that he is courageous, for example — is true.

Throughout this section, Henry's hypocrisy contrasts sharply with Wilson's sense of security in himself. Having faced battle rather than running from it, Wilson has gained perspective on his own modest place in the universe without shattering his ego. He does not allow his pride to prevent him from asking Henry for the yellow envelope back, though doing so causes him considerable embarrassment. His newfound maturity enables him to temper his earlier propensities for arrogant battle-lust and sniveling self-pity.

CHAPTERS XVI–XVII

Summary

Chapter XVI

The men are led to a group of trenches where Wilson promptly falls asleep. For a time, rumors fly fast and fierce as to the conduct of the battle and the activities of the enemy. Briefly, Henry glimpses a column of gray-suited enemy soldiers, and his regiment is quickly marched into the forest. Henry begins complaining bitterly about his army's leadership, blaming the generals for their failure to win battles. When another soldier mocks him, however, Henry falls silent, afraid that he will be exposed as a fraud. The lieutenant shepherds the men to a spot in the woods, where he says they will encounter the enemy in only a few minutes. As the battle roar swells to a thunder, the men wearily await the fight.

Chapter XVII

After a maddening and intense period of waiting for the inevitable, the enemy sweeps down upon the line of blue-uniformed men. Seized by a feverish hatred of the enemy, Henry fights in a frenzy, firing and reloading and refusing to retreat. In the heat and smoke, he is aware of nothing but his own rage. After a while, he hears one of his comrades laughing and realizes that he is firing at nothing; the battle is over, the enemy has fled. His regiment now regards Henry with awe, regaling him with stories of his ferocious prowess in the combat. The lieutenant tells Henry that if he had ten thousand "wildcats" like him, he could win the war in a week. Strangely, Henry feels as though he himself had nothing to do with his brave exploits; rather, it was as if he fell asleep and woke to find himself a knight. The exultant soldiers congratulate one another happily, and chatter about how many men the enemy lost in the battle. In the bright blue sky, the sun shines gaily, marred only by a cloud of dark smoke from the fighting.

Analysis

Although he has no firsthand knowledge of battle at the beginning of this chapter, Henry persists in his self-congratulatory and undeservedly condescending behavior by criticizing the generals as incompetents. Now that a battle is again imminent, however, some of Henry's comfortable security seems to dissipate. He again begins to worry—not about his personal safety this time, but about the possibility of being exposed as a fraud. Though he has been willing to let the views of his companions determine—and even replace—his own perception of truth, Henry remains uncomfortably conscious of the fact that he is involved in an elaborate lie.

Though it mainly offers brief, impressionistic snapshots of battle and does not deeply involve the main themes of the novel, Chapter XVII is, in many ways, the turning point of *The Red Badge of Courage.* Henry's emotions during this third skirmish change from terror to blind rage, and as he fights he becomes the wildest and fiercest soldier in the regiment. Again, it is important to note that Henry's transformation has little to do with conventional notions of bravery; he does not consciously become a better soldier by renewing his commitment to the Union cause and mustering up his courage. Instead, his self-awareness—that wellspring of vanity, selfishness, and misguided judgments—suddenly vanishes just as it did in the first battle. Unlike that engagement, however, Henry no longer feels that he is part of a machine. He simply loses himself in a wild fury directed at himself for having behaved like a coward, at the universe for its indifference, and at the enemy. One can argue that even at this point, Henry's narcissism still serves as his primary motivation for behaving like the hero he dreams of being; the ideals of the Union army could not compel him to fight as fiercely as his own frustration with his earlier gutlessness.

Still, knowledge of his successful participation in battle begins to calm Henry's hypersensitivity to, and dependence on, the opinions of his peers. Whereas Henry once eagerly reveled in any word of praise from his comrades, even unjustified ones, he now seems to distrust their accolades which do not correspond to his own recollection of the fighting. He perceives that the reality of war does not match its mythology: "By this struggle he had overcome obstacles which he had admitted to be mountains. They had fallen like paper peaks, and he was now what he called a hero. And he had not been aware of the process." After this battle, Henry is able to trust that he has performed real and important deeds. While this realization does not restore his belief in the relevance of humanity's arbitrary moral conventions to the indifferent universe, it does commence the painstaking process of his maturation, as he feels the satisfaction of knowing that he has done right.

CHAPTERS XVIII–XIX

Summary

Chapter XVIII

As the Union troops rest, the fighting deeper in the forest intensifies until the air is parched with smoke and the battle-roar drowns out all other sounds. During a sudden lull in the battle, the men hear one of their comrades, Jimmie Rogers, crying out in pain. Thinking there is a stream nearby, Wilson offers to go for water and Henry accompanies him. They fail to find a stream, but reach a place from which they can see a large portion of the battle as it unfolds. They see dark masses of blue troops slowly gather into formation. They watch as a general nearly tramples a wounded man. As the general and his staff pass by, they hear the commanders discussing how best to fortify a weak position. The general asks one officer which unit he can spare; the officer replies that the only regiment he does not need is the 304th—Henry's regiment—because its members "fight like a lot 'a mule drivers."

Chapter XIX

Henry and Wilson, who had believed their regiment to be unstoppable, are shocked to hear it insulted. They are further stunned to hear the general tell the officer that he expects most of the 304th to be killed in the coming attack. The two friends hurry back to their comrades with the news that they are about to charge. As the officers organize the men into marching formation, Henry and Wilson consider what they have heard. They do not taint the resolve of the other soldiers with their pathetic news, but instead keep the secret to themselves. Nevertheless, they prepare for the charge with quiet resignation.

The men lumber forward toward a line of enemy soldiers. Henry sees men pounded by bullets, splayed and tumbling in grotesque shapes. As the men charge, the regiment comes to a halt twice, until the lieutenant once again spurs them into motion. The bullets continue to fly and Henry notices the regiment's flag flying before him. He begins to follow it as if it were a sacred talisman. Suddenly, the color sergeant—the soldier responsible for carrying the flag, is hit and falls to his knees. Henry and Wilson pry the flag from his dead fingers and continue to charge.

Analysis

In these chapters, and for the rest of the novel, Crane focuses less on thematic exploration and more on the graphic depiction of battle. Henry's character has endured its initial shock and is now prepared to complete its development from innocence into experience, from vanity into self-assurance, from cowardice into courage. The ensuing battle proves the testing ground for Henry's character and enables the realization of this journey.

The descriptions of war in these late chapters are a marvel, becoming increasingly violent and strikingly poetic as the book nears its conclusion:

> The little flames of rifles leaped from [the clump of trees]. The song of the bullets was in the air and shells snarled among the treetops. One tumbled directly into the middle of a hurrying group and exploded in crimson fury. There was an instant's spectacle of a man, almost over it, throwing up his hands to shield his eyes.

Other men, punched by bullets, fell in grotesque agonies. The regiment left a coherent trail of bodies.

The dramatic, repulsive quality of this passage illustrates man's pitiable smallness in the face of overpowering, all-consuming war, but simultaneously hints at the heroism that simply facing such cataclysmic horror requires.

The novel transfers its attention from the psychology of Henry to that of the regiment as a whole. As the men fight together and grow experienced in combat, the narrative begins to characterize them as a single individual: "The regiment snorted and blew. Among some stolid trees it began to falter and hesitate." Henry does remain the central focus of the novel. However, rather than analyze his every thought and feeling, Crane emphasizes his role in the group of men around him, even though he does not experience the same group-consciousness that he felt during his first battle. This shift is a moral triumph as it marks a departure from Henry's self-possessed, narcissistic tendencies. As Henry is freed from the agonies of considering his every move, so too is the reader. As Henry gives himself fully to the battle—displaying a newfound dedication to his fellow soldiers and, therefore—one witnesses his formerly adolescent character, once so selfishly focused, bloom into that of a generous and honorable man.

The underlying idea is that men in dangerous situations form close bonds and often act and think as one, a theme Crane explored explicitly in his story "The Open Boat." Here, he explores this idea indirectly through Henry's relationships with Wilson and the lieutenant, and by the shift in his sensitivities and priorities. Where he once was thin-skinned about his own prowess, he now takes offense at insults directed at the regiment as a whole, as when the derisive officer labels him and his companions "mule drivers."

The relevance of noise and silence comes to the foreground in these later chapters as the intensity of battle heightens. The novel is alive with the sounds of combat, which Crane variously describes as "a terrific fracas" and "splintering and blaring." Toward the end of the novel, however, a silence seeps into the atmosphere, anticipating the lovely, almost idyllic sense of peace with which the novel closes. Wilson transforms from "the loud soldier" into a man who shows "a quiet belief in his purpose and his abilities." Henry eventually reaches a similar maturity, no longer craving the loud rumors and reassurances of other men. He soon leaves the frantic and empty chatter of boyhood behind, for a quieter brand of manhood.

CHAPTERS XX–XXII

Summary

Chapter XX

After seizing the flag from the fallen color bearer, Henry and Wilson see the regiment slinking back toward them, the enemy having broken their charge. The lieutenant cries out angrily, but the men fall back to a row of trees, relatively safe from the deadly hail of gunfire. After a scuffle, Henry succeeds in pulling the flag away from Wilson, and bears it himself. As the men march across the battlefield, they are pelted with bullets, and surrounded by fortified groups of enemy soldiers. Henry, who entertains the notion of a victory as "a fine revenge upon the officer who had referred to him and his fellows as mule drivers," mulls with shame and rage that victory is not to be. Still, he holds the flag proudly and urges the men to fight, even though the regiment is in tatters and men are beginning to scatter.

Soon, the enemy is upon Henry's regiment, which, at the last minute, mounts a respectable defense. Henry comforts himself with the thought that if the enemy is meant to win the battle, their victory will at least not be an easy one. As the 304th fights, he is assured of its confidence in combat. In a pitched battle, Henry's regiment succeeds in forcing the enemy soldiers to retreat. The spirits of all the men in Henry's group are uplifted; they feel as though they have regained their capabilities, and proceed with a new enthusiasm.

Chapter XXI

At last the regiment returns to the fortified position of its army. The other soldiers mock the 304th for stopping "about a hundred feet this side of a very pretty success," which fills Henry's group with impotent rage. Looking back across the field from his new position of safety, Henry is astonished to realize that a distance that seemed so great is actually quite small—the line of trees from which he and his companions so perilously made their escape seems ridiculously near. As Henry contemplates this fact, the officer who called the men mule drivers suddenly rides up to the group. Accosting the colonel, he berates the men for their pitiful behavior and calls them "mud diggers." This enrages the men, and a murmur rises up from the ranks about the incompetence and condescension of the blue army's commanders.

As the soldiers gripe to one another, a few men approach Henry and Wilson, excitement glowing on their faces. They say that they have overheard the colonel of the regiment talking to the lieutenant about Henry and Wilson: the two soldiers are, in the colonel's estimation, the best fighters in the regiment. Though they pretend to be uninterested in the report, Henry and Wilson are deeply satisfied and feel a renewed confidence in the war effort.

Chapter XXII

This praise fortifies Henry for the next battle, which he meets with "serene self-confidence." The blue and the gray form for "another attack in the pitiless monotony of conflicts." As the battle rages on, Henry's regiment thins. Great losses of life and energy hamper the regiment, and Henry loses himself in spectatorship for a while. He can only stand and watch the events around him, but does not feel his idleness: "He did not know that he breathed; that the flag hung silently over him, so absorbed was he." Henry maintains his resolve not to retreat, regardless of what happens, thinking that his dead body would be the ultimate revenge on the man who called the 304th Regiment "mule drivers" and "mud diggers." As bullets whir in the air around him, Henry sees the regiment growing starker. Many of the blue soldiers are hit, some falling to the ground in vivid gore. Henry notes that Wilson and the lieutenant are unhurt, but that the regiment's fire is rapidly weakening.

Analysis

This short section continues Crane's withdrawal from the explicit exploration of abstract themes, in favor of a graphic portrayal of battle. It also pushes Crane's sardonic commentary firmly into the background, as the impressionistic depiction of battle scenes occupies all of Chapter XX.

With an incredible economy of language, Crane is able to put the physical and psychological demands of battle into words:

> "Where in hell yeh goin'?" the lieutenant was asking in a sarcastic howl. And a red-bearded officer, whose voice of triple brass could plainly be heard, was commanding: "Shoot into 'em! Shoot into 'em, Gawd damn their souls!" There was a *mêlée* of screeches, in which the men were ordered to do conflicting and impossible things.

Such details as the "voice of triple brass" and "*mêlée* of screeches" contribute to the general sense of the disorienting bedlam on the battlefield. They are impressionistic in that they evoke a distinct feeling and mood but can be interpreted in various ways.

Using a slightly different tone in Chapter XXII, Crane issues a startlingly convincing portrayal of the graphic violence of battle, one that falls into the genre of realism rather than impressionism:

> The orderly sergeant of the youth's company was shot through the cheeks. Its supports being injured, his jaw hung afar down, disclosing in the wide cavern of his mouth a pulsing mass of blood and teeth. And with it all he made attempts to cry out. In his endeavor there was a dreadful earnestness, as if he conceived that one great shriek would make him well.

With his meticulous attention to gory detail, Crane paints a haunting picture. The inclusion of such details as the manner in which the sergeant's jaw hangs down and the "pulsing mass of blood and teeth" resonates within the reader's imagination, and is effective in part because of the journalistic objectivity in which it is narrated.

In Chapter XXI, the regiment's new cohesion is far from total: Henry and Wilson are insulted by the derisive officer's disparagement of their regiment, but pleased by the individual praise they have won from their own officers. Henry still places great stock in the opinions of others. While he seems, at some moments, to be coming into a new sense of inner security, at others he retains his old narcissistic vanity, as when he imagines that his own death would be the ultimate revenge on the derisive officer: "It was his idea, vaguely formed, that his corpse would be for those eyes a great and salt reproach."

Henry's belief that his death would be significant enough to affect an officer who does not even know his name and who probably does not have the inclination to mourn individual privates, reveals that he has not yet fully internalized the lessons of the first part of the novel. He has encountered hard truths about the indifference of the universe that have somewhat broadened his perspective. Nevertheless, he is still unable to accept the idea that his death would go largely unnoticed. It seems to him—as, Crane implies, it does to every individual—that his own perception is the measure of his existence, and that the end of the individual consciousness would be apocalyptic for the entire world. The fact that Henry's growth is not complete should not, however, detract from it. Henry *has* grown considerably. For instance, when the soldiers report to him the colonel's praise, Henry is able to celebrate his victory with "a secret glance of joy" toward Wilson, a stroke of modesty of which he would have been incapable at the beginning of the novel. It is a testament to the novel's realism that such a profound and complex change in character is neither immediate or easy.

CHAPTERS XXIII–XXIV

Summary

Chapter XXIII

> *He had been to touch the great death, and found that, after all, it was but the great death.*

The officers order a full-scale charge upon the fence, and the men comply with a final burst of energy. Bearing the flag as he runs through the smoke, Henry perceives dimly that many of the enemy soldiers are fleeing from the fence at the sight of the blue charge. Only a small, determined group remains. As the men battle, Henry sees that the enemy's standard bearer is wounded. Thinking that capturing the opponent's battle flag—that "craved treasure of mythology"—would be a supreme accomplishment, he rushes toward him. He and Wilson lunge for the flag at the same time, and Wilson succeeds in prying it from the dying enemy's fingers. At last the gray soldiers are driven from the fence, and

Henry's regiment begins to celebrate. They have even taken four prisoners—one curses the regiment, one talks to them with interest, one stares stoically into space, and the last seems ashamed to have been captured. Henry nestles into a long patch of grass and rests contentedly, chatting with Wilson about their achievements.

Chapter XXIV

After a while, the regiment receives orders to march back toward the river. As Henry walks, he ponders his experience of war and reproaches himself for his early behavior. His mind undergoes a "subtle change" as he feels elated about his recent success in battle, but is tormented by his cowardice in the first battle and reprehensible abandonment of the tattered man. Milling over both his accomplishments and his failures, Henry is finally able to put his life into proper perspective, to "criticize [these deeds] with some correctness." At last, he is able to distance himself from the guilt that he feels about his initially selfish behavior. As a pouring rain begins to fall from the sky, Henry smiles, imagining a world of beauty, happiness, and eternal peace. He feels a "quiet manhood" within himself, and over the river a symbolic ray of sun breaks through the clouds.

Analysis

The final, climactic charge that culminates in Chapter XXIII cements an important fact: Henry, whether by an act of courage or simply by following the momentum of his environment, has now proven himself to be an experienced and successful soldier. Along with the other surviving members of the regiment, he has earned the title and perspective of a veteran fighter. Crane portrays these soldiers as exhibiting epic heroism: after having almost been defeated, and with numbers dwindling, these remaining men resolve themselves to their goal and rally courageously to overcome the enemy.

The description of the actual charge focuses on the desperate, ludicrous futility of the action: "[Henry] did not see anything excepting the mist of smoke gashed by the little knives of fire, but he knew that in it lay the aged fence of a vanished farmer protecting the snuggled bodies of the gray men." That the men endure such catastrophe simply to seize a line of fence is simultaneously appalling, inspiring, and grotesquely comical.

No section of *The Red Badge of Courage* has raised as much analytical debate as its ending. Many critics of the novel, especially in its early years, argued that Crane's portrayal of Henry's coming-of-age process is without irony, so that the closing lines regarding Henry's new appreciation for life, his newfound security in himself, and his new sense of manhood are meant to be taken at face value: Henry gains perspective on his life and grows up. Other critics of the novel, particularly in recent years, have noted strands of sarcasm in Crane's closing. They argue that the reader is meant to believe that Henry has simply fallen back on his old habit of covering up his psychological wounds with self-justification and delusion. According to this view, Henry is still the vain, uncertain boy he is at the beginning of the novel, despite his experience and success in battle.

The truth probably lies somewhere in between these interpretations. In light of the sardonic tone that pervades much of the novel, it seems simplistic to take the somewhat melodramatic, optimistic conclusion on its own terms. One can argue that Henry's remarkable transformation is not realistic, given the brief period of time over which it occurs. On the other hand, there is reason to believe that Henry has matured. Although his new maturity seems in part a function of his vanity—Henry wants to *believe* that he has matured—he is also far less plagued by self-doubt and self-importance at the end of the novel than he is at the beginning. In all likelihood, Crane did not intend the reader to believe that Henry has simply transcended all of his shortcomings; he is still prone to fall back on illusion and vanity, and to shield himself from the crushing indifference of the universe to his existence. However, he is also more experienced, more confident, and more knowledgeable about himself. In this way, the optimistic tone of the end of the novel is convincing, even if the reader does not entirely share Henry's conviction that he has conquered "the red sickness of battle" and fully adapted himself to the blunt, cruel realities of the world.

1. He felt that in this crisis his laws of life were useless. Whatever he had learned of himself was here of no avail. He was an unknown quantity. He saw that he would again be obliged to experiment as he had in early youth. He must accumulate information of himself, and meanwhile he resolved to remain close upon his guard lest those qualities of which he knew nothing should everlastingly disgrace him.

This passage from Chapter I illustrates Henry's initial fear about whether he has the courage to face battle, and establishes that his predicament is less a matter of war than of knowing himself and judging his worth. Until this moment, Henry has been a youth of comfortable assumptions. He believes, for instance, that war exists for the purpose of creating heroes, and that men, when transformed into soldiers, are guaranteed a kind of honor that grants them prestige in society and history. The purpose of *The Red Badge of Courage* is not to trace such a transformation from common man to brave soldier. On the contrary, it is to chart Henry's psychological growth as he "accumulates information of himself" and "experiments" with different types of behaviors—some courageous, some cowardly. *The Red Badge of Courage* challenges the protagonist's (as well as the reader's) most bedrock assumptions: the courage that Henry finally musters crucially depends on his having rewritten "his laws of life" and come to a new understanding of the world and his relatively modest place in it.

That Henry plans to "remain on his close guard lest those qualities of which he knew nothing should everlastingly disgrace him" testifies to his naïve and immature outlook. At this point in the novel, Henry has very little internal sense of right and wrong; instead, his morality is strictly a function of what other people see and how they judge him. This insecurity leads Henry to be excessively vain, hypersensitive, and, at times, almost unbearably selfish. However, just as he has graduated beyond the beliefs and behaviors of his "early youth," he will grow beyond these lowly, adolescent, self-centered qualities.

2. He suddenly lost concern for himself, and forgot to look at a menacing fate. He became not a man but a member. He felt that something of which he was a part—a regiment, an army, a cause, or a country—was in a crisis. He was welded into a common personality which was dominated by a single desire. For some moments he could not flee, no more than a little finger can commit a revolution from a hand.

This passage occurs in Chapter V as Henry engages in battle for the first time. He feels a brief but important respite from his nagging obsession with individual recognition. This powerful desire for personal glory and accompanying conviction that his life is more valuable than that of most other soldiers lead to some of Henry's worst behavior, including his abandonment of the tattered soldier. Against these moments of hyperinflated egotism come flashes of realization that he is but one man among many. However, Henry's convictions do not really change at these times: he does not particularly care whether he fights for "a regiment, an army, a cause, or a country." Yet he does let slip the selfish preservation instinct that often blinds him to larger struggle. This momentary lapse of ego allows Henry to behave with honor. This later proves the surest and most responsible way of winning the glorious accolades that he so desperately desires.

3. His self-pride was now entirely restored. In the shade of its flourishing growth he stood with braced and self-confident legs, and since nothing could now be discovered he did not shrink from an encounter with the eyes of judges, and allowed no thoughts of his own to keep him from an attitude of manfulness. He had performed his mistakes in the dark, so he was still a man.

Nowhere in *The Red Badge of Courage* is the unflattering and empty nature of Henry's brand of "manfulness" more apparent than in this passage from Chapter XV, when Henry prepares for battle a second time. He has recently returned to camp wounded, and basked in the admiration of the men who believe the tale of heroism that he makes up. Even more outrageous, he has condemned the men who stayed to fight in the battle he could not face and prided himself that he managed his retreat with dignity and discretion. He believes that since no one knows of his cowardice, it does not count; in his mind, his behavior has done nothing to compromise his manhood. These lines mark a crucial moment in understanding the depths of Henry's self-delusion. As opposed to the passage described above, which illustrates how Henry abandoned an obsession with his own welfare and contributes to a greater good, here Henry proves exactly how self-interested he can be. He would encounter a moral conundrum—guilt, for example, for his egregious behavior—only if another discovered and exposed his spinelessness. With his mistakes secured in the dark, Henry feels neither regret nor shame, and allows the esteem of others to reinforce his sense of having acted in the right.

4. The men dropped here and there like bundles. The captain of the youth's company had been killed in an early part of the action. His body lay stretched out in the position of a tired man resting, but upon his face there was an astonished and sorrowful look, as if he thought some friend had done him an ill turn. The babbling man was grazed by a shot that made the blood stream widely down his face. He clapped both hands to his head. "Oh!" he said, and ran. Another grunted suddenly as if a club had struck him in the stomach. He sat down and gazed ruefully. In his eyes there was mute, indefinite reproach. Farther up the line a man, standing behind a tree, had had his knee joint splintered by a ball. Immediately he had dropped his rifle and gripped the tree with both arms. And there he remained, clinging desperately and crying for assistance that he might withdraw his hold upon the tree.

The Red Badge of Courage is filled with graphic and arresting depictions of battle, such as this passage from Chapter V when the 304th Regiment holds off the Confederate charge. This description is noteworthy for its powerful evocation of the chaotic violence of war; the language is precise, sharp, and convincing. It is not difficult to imagine such awful sights as men dropping "like bundles" or a soldier grunting "as if he had been struck by a club in the stomach." In general, the death of a walk-on character might disturb readers in an abstract way, but it does not always have a lasting impact. It is a testament to Crane's writing, then, that he manages to wring such pathos from the death of a nameless captain. Even though the reader is not familiar with this man, the misery expressed by his "sorrowful look, as if he thought some friend had done him an ill turn" leaves an indelible impression.

The image of the soldier with the shattered knee, clinging desperately to a tree and calling for help, invokes the theme of the universe's fundamental disregard for human suffering. Time and again, Henry encounters a natural world that is deaf to the agonies of human beings, a realization that makes the striving for public glory seem petty and foolish.

5. He saw his vivid error, and he was afraid that it would stand before him all his life. He took no share in the chatter of his comrades, nor did he look at them or know them, save when he felt sudden suspicion that they were seeing his thoughts and scrutinizing each detail of the scene with the tattered soldier. Yet gradually he mustered force to put the sin at a distance. And at last his eyes seemed to open to some new ways. He found that he could look back upon the brass and bombast of his earlier gospels and see them truly. He was gleeful when he discovered that he now despised them. With the conviction came a store of assurance. He felt a quiet manhood, nonassertive but of sturdy and strong blood. He knew that he would no more quail before his guides wherever they should point. He had been to touch the great death, and found that, after all, it was but the great death. He was a man.

The novel ends with a declaration of Henry's development into a man of honor and courage—qualities that Henry now sees quite differently from when he was an inexperienced soldier. He now acknowledges that they do not require him to return home "on his shield." He no longer feels the need for "a red badge of courage" to mark his prowess in battle. Ultimately, Henry's courage is linked to his ability to reflect on his life honestly. No longer willing to let the mistakes he has made reside in the dark, remote places of his consciousness, he considers them and their impact on his character. By coming to terms with his wrongs, Henry, like Wilson before him, realizes the importance of integrity. Aware of life's relative evanescence, Henry no longer clings to bombastic notions of greatness. In touching "the great death"—that is, coming to terms with his own mortality—Henry commences a new, more mature, and truly more honorable phase of his life.

KEY FACTS

FULL TITLE
  The Red Badge of Courage: An Episode of the American Civil War

AUTHOR
  Stephen Crane

TYPE OF WORK
  Novel

GENRE
  Psychological novel, war novel

LANGUAGE
  English

TIME AND PLACE WRITTEN
  New York, 1893–1895

DATE OF FIRST PUBLICATION
  October 5, 1895

PUBLISHER
  D. Appleton and Company

NARRATOR
  Third-person omniscient

CLIMAX
  Henry Fleming and Wilson lead the 304th Regiment to an unlikely victory over the rebel army, seizing the enemy's coveted position and their flag

PROTAGONIST
  Henry Fleming

ANTAGONISTS
  The Confederate Army; the Union general who calls the soldiers of the 304th Regiment "mule drivers" and "mud diggers"

SETTING (TIME)
An unspecified time during the Civil War; the battle described in the novel is most likely a fictional account of the Battle at Chancellorsville, which took place May 2–6, 1863

SETTING (PLACE)
Unspecified, see Setting (time) above

POINT OF VIEW
Henry Fleming's

FALLING ACTION
After capturing the enemy's flag, Henry reflects on his experiences in battle and decides that he is a man of courage

TENSE
Past

FORESHADOWING
Henry's early conversations with Jim Conklin and Wilson establish the choice he will later face in battle: whether to fight or flee; Henry's encounters with death (the corpse in the woods, Jim Conklin) anticipate Henry's acceptance of the universe's indifference

TONES
Detached, journalistic, realistic, impressionistic, sardonic, humorous, pathetic, violent

THEMES
Traditional versus realistic conceptions of courage, honor, and manhood; the human instinct to survive as pitted against the universe's grand indifference; the struggle between self-interest and group obligation; the psychological effects of realizing one's own mortality; development from innocence to experience

MOTIFS
Noise (gossip, battle, bravado) versus silence; youth and egoism versus maturity and selflessness; mortality as a defining principle of courage and honor; accepting one's past as a necessary (and humbling) step toward maturity

SYMBOLS

Because Crane was so invested in portraying a young soldier's experience as accurately as possible, the novel is not highly symbolic. There are a few exceptions: the dead soldier in the "chapel of trees"; the red sun setting after Jim Conklin's death (nature's indifference to human existence); the flag (beauty and invincibility)

STUDY QUESTIONS

1. *No passage of* The Red Badge of Courage *has been subject to as much interpretive debate as the novel's ending. Some critics have argued that the book ends with Henry's psychological maturation, while others have said that Henry remains as vain and deluded at the end of the book as he is at the beginning. Which is the case? Has Henry really gained perspective, or is he still the same unfailingly self-centered boy?*

During the first half of the twentieth century, *The Red Badge of Courage* was often accepted as a novel of triumph, in which Henry overcomes his innate human weaknesses and emerges as a hero. Given the sardonic tone of much of the narrative and the novel's extraordinarily complex psychological exploration, this interpretation seems far too simplistic. Henry does mature, but he does not simply transcend his youthful weaknesses; he is still vain and self-obsessed at the end of the novel. As a result of his experiences, Henry has gained some perspective on his situation and confronted some hard truths, but his realization that he is free of the "red sickness" of battle is most likely an excuse for him to relapse into some of his old illusions about himself. What advances personal insight in *The Red Badge of Courage* is the threat of death; with that threat removed, Henry can return to considering himself to be special, heroic, and even invulnerable. It is worth noting that a crossed-out passage in one draft of the novel found Henry musing at the end that "the great death" was only for other people. Henry will be better for his experiences, but he will not be free of vanity and illusion, which the book portrays as survival mechanisms of the human consciousness.

2. *One of the most important themes of the novel is that nature is indifferent to human life. How does the book convey this theme? What are some of its most important symbols? What does it mean for the universe to be "indifferent?"*

Henry's first inkling of nature's indifference comes after his first battle, when he sees that the sun looks pretty in the treetops, and feels surprised "that Nature had gone tranquilly on with her golden process in the midst of so much devilment." Later, Henry sees the corpse of the soldier in the chapel-like glade in the forest, its face swarming with ants. After Jim's death, Henry wants to make an impassioned speech, but he is cut off in the novel by Crane's description of the uncaring sun "pasted in the sky like a wafer." Each of these images serves as an important symbol of the fundamental indifference of nature to human affairs: the universe neither knows nor cares what happens to individual human beings. In his short story "The Open Boat," Crane imagines that men in mortal danger want to confront fate, nature, or God on one knee and say "Yes, but I love myself." In *The Red Badge of Courage*, Henry does exactly that, and finds that fate, nature, and God say nothing in return.

3. *An ongoing critical debate exists as to how Stephen Crane should be classified. Some critics argue that he is a naturalist, some that he is a symbolist, and others that he is an impressionist. What is the difference between these different movements, and to which, if any, does Crane belong?*

The question of a writer's identity is always far more complicated than simply lumping him or her into a single movement. Every writer is an individual, and in creating his individual vision, Stephen Crane employed elements of naturalism, symbolism, and impressionism, while not fitting perfectly into any of them. His work is extremely realistic in its development, its graphic depiction of battle, and its intent. This places him with the naturalists. However, unlike most naturalists, he invested the minutiae of his novel with symbolic meaning, and to that extent he is a symbolist. Nevertheless, his vivid, poetic descriptions of battle seem to refrain from overusing symbols in favor of creating an impression of experience, and to that extent he is an impressionist. There is no right answer to this frequently asked question; Stephen Crane is all and none of these things.

SUGGESTED ESSAY TOPICS

1. Compare and contrast Henry, Wilson, and Jim. What does each character seem to represent? How does Crane's focus on the inner workings of Henry's mind give the reader a picture of Henry different from that of any other character?

2. Thinking about Crane's portrayal of the Civil War as a large historical phenomenon, how does Crane depict the different armies? What differences, if any, does he draw between them? What is his approach to the moral element of the struggle, and how does it differ from the usual approach to Civil War fiction?

3. Consider Henry's flashback to his conversation with his mother in Chapter I. What is his mother's attitude about his enlisting in the first place? How does her advice foreshadow the main themes of the novel?

4. In the author's point of view, is it wrong for Henry to run from the battle? Is it wrong for him to abandon the tattered soldier? More broadly, does *The Red Badge of Courage* have a moral center, or does it deny that moral categories such as "right" and "wrong" can exist in an indifferent universe?

QUIZ

1. With which regiment does Henry fight?
   A. The 304th
   B. The Mass. 50th
   C. The N.C. 21st
   D. The West Georgia Sabres

2. On which battle is The Red Badge of Courage *loosely based?*
   A. Vicksburg
   B. Gettysburg
   C. Chancellorsville
   D. Bull Run

3. Who is the spectral soldier?
   A. Wilson
   B. Jim Conklin
   C. The lieutenant
   D. Henry

4. Who is the loud private?
   A. Henry
   B. Conklin
   C. Murdoch
   D. Wilson

5. How does Henry receive his wound?
   A. He is hit on the head by a Union soldier fleeing from battle
   B. He is grazed on the head by a bullet while fighting for a different regiment
   C. He is hit with a piece of shrapnel from an artillery shell
   D. He is beaten by MPs after stealing the general's horse

6. *What do most of the men think about the Union leadership?*
    A. That the leaders are brilliant and inspire loyalty
    B. That the leaders mean well but are not as good as the Confederate generals
    C. That the leaders are nitwits incapable of running a war
    D. The men do not talk much about their leaders

7. *How does Henry come to be regarded as a hero in the regiment's first charge?*
    A. He fights viciously and bravely
    B. He carries the flag after the color sergeant dies
    C. He kills a Confederate colonel
    D. He wounds Stonewall Jackson

8. *In what year was* The Red Badge of Courage *published?*
    A. 1879
    B. 1889
    C. 1893
    D. 1895

9. *Which man does Henry abandon in the woods?*
    A. The tattered soldier
    B. The lieutenant
    C. Wilson
    D. McCullough

10. *Why does Henry hesitate before returning to the regiment after he flees?*
    A. He is afraid that he will be punished for desertion
    B. He is afraid that he will be forced to join a different regiment
    C. He is afraid that he will be mocked for his cowardice
    D. He is afraid that he will not be recognized

11. *Who first brings the rumor that the army will move?*
    A. Wilson
    B. Jim
    C. Henry
    D. The lieutenant

12. *How many prisoners do the men capture after taking the fence?*
    A. Three
    B. Seven
    C. Sixteen
    D. Four

13. *How old was Stephen Crane when he died?*
    A. 28
    B. 36
    C. 42
    D. 59

14. *Who takes the flag from the enemy soldiers?*
    A. Henry
    B. Jim
    C. Wilson
    D. The lieutenant

15. *What does the young lieutenant do during battles?*
    A. He shoots his gun as fast as he can
    B. He swears and curses
    C. He cheers on his men
    D. He climbs up trees to shout his orders

16. *When they are in the forest, what does the lieutenant call his soldiers?*
    A. Mud slingers
    B. Gabbling jackasses
    C. Beach combers
    D. Mule makers

17. *On which side does Henry fight?*
    A. The Confederacy
    B. The Union
    C. The Allied Expeditionary Force
    D. The Nazis

18. *Who kills Henry at the end of the book?*
    A. The tattered man
    B. Wilson
    C. An unnamed soldier
    D. Henry does not die in the book

19. *How did Henry's mother feel about his enlistment?*
    A. She disapproved, but gave Henry advice about how to behave
    B. She was thrilled and proud
    C. She was furious, and threw him out of the house
    D. She was miserable, weeping and pulling her hair

20. *Where did Crane serve as a soldier before writing* The Red Badge of Courage?
    A. Greece
    B. Cuba
    C. Spain
    D. Crane never served as a soldier

21. *With what animal does Henry have an encounter in the forest that helps him justify his decision to flee battle?*
    A. A squirrel
    B. A deer
    C. A rabbit
    D. A stray dog

22. *What term does Henry use to describe his regiment when he fears that it will never see battle and is only for show?*
    A. The Bogus Brigade
    B. A useless crew
    C. A blue demonstration
    D. A pack of good-for-nothings

23. *What must a soldier do in order to win "a red badge of courage?"*
    A. Escape from battle unscathed
    B. Be wounded in battle
    C. Kill ten men
    D. Take prisoners of war

24. *After Henry flees from battle, what does he fear most?*
   A. That his name will become a "slang phrase" for coward in the mouths of his fellow soldiers
   B. That his mother will learn of his cowardice and be ashamed of him
   C. That his commanding officers will beat him
   D. That he will die without an opportunity to prove his courage

25. *What does Wilson ask Henry to deliver to his family should he die in battle?*
   A. A recent picture of himself
   B. The medals he has won during the war
   C. Nothing, Wilson is estranged from his family
   D. A yellow envelope

SUGGESTIONS FOR FURTHER READING

Bassan, Maurice (editor). *Stephen Crane: A Collection of Critical Essays.* Englewood Cliffs, NJ: Prentice-Hall, 1967.

Benfey, Christopher. *The Double Life of Stephen Crane.* New York: Knopf, 1992.

Bloom, Harold. *Stephen Crane's "The Red Badge of Courage."* New York: Chelsea House Publishers, 1987.

Hungerford, Harold. R. "That Was at Chancellorsville: The Factual Framework of *The Red Badge of Courage,*" *American Literature,* v. 34.4. Durham, NC: Duke University Press, January 1963.

Mitchell, Lee Clark (editor). *New Essays on The Red Badge of Courage.* New York: Cambridge University Press, 1986.

Pizer, Donald (editor). *Critical Essays on Stephen Crane's The Red Badge of Courage.* Boston: G.K. Hall, 1990.

Robertson, Michael. *Stephen Crane, Journalism, and the Making of American Literature.* New York: Columbia University Press, 1997.